Kids Without Mom

whispers of love, oodles of hugs,
biblical truths and real life lessons
for kids without mom

✳ ✳ ✳

Vanessa Nartey

Scriptures taken from the Holy Bible, New International Version®, NIV®. Copyright © 1973, 1978, 1984, 2011 by Biblica, Inc.™ Used by permission of Zondervan. All rights reserved worldwide. www.zondervan.com The "NIV" and "New International Version" are trademarks registered in the United States Patent and Trademark Office by Biblica, Inc.™ Copyright ©

2014 by Vanessa Nartey.

All rights reserved. No part of this publication may be reproduced, distributed or transmitted in any form or by any means, including photocopying, recording, or other electronic or mechanical methods, without the prior written per-mission of the publisher, except in the case of brief quotations embodied in critical reviews and certain other noncommercial uses permitted by copyright law. For permission requests, write to the publisher, addressed "Attention: Permissions Coordinator," at the address below.

Vanessa Nartey/Joy In The Story Publishing
1500 Farmer Rd. Suite F-1
Conyers, GA/30012

www.joyinthestory.com

Ordering Information: Special discounts are available on quantity purchases by not for profit organizations, child care associations, and others. For details, contact the publisher at info@joyinthestory.com.

Atlanta / Vanessa Nartey — Second Edition

ISBN-13: 978-1497596801
ISBN-10: 1497596807
Printed in the United States of America

Dedication

To my husband Daniel who does more than any wife should dare ask and my daughters Cynthia and Naakie, the most patient, forgiving and gracious girls I know.

To My Mother

At times the emotions are so intense that I just have to stand still and let wonder have its way.

What color were your eyes? Would we have been best friends or distant? How did you laugh? Were you funny or serious? How did you wear your hair?

The questions about you will always remain whispered wonderings. But when I listen closely, put my face to the wind, I hear - in the breaking forth of spring flowers from wintered ground, birds' outstretched glides, and the autumn sway of tree leaves – one undeniably beautiful answer…the birthed beat of my heart.

Thank you mom...

May you, reader of this book, discover love in the fact that you were born.

For Someone Special

If your mother has died or she is not in your life at the moment, you probably have many questions about her and about yourself.

The loss of a mother is one that cannot be replaced by anyone or anything else. If you were very young when she left your life and do not remember much about her, perhaps you can share in the memories of her friends and family.

Facts about your mom – how she wore her hair, if she liked to cook, or a nickname she gave to you, become treasures when she is no longer with you. Remembering can make you feel her love all over again, or can fill you with a longing to see her and have her in your life. Be honest with your feelings. When the memories make you smile and laugh, smile and laugh big and loud. When they make you feel as though your heart is being pulled apart, cry until the tugging of your heart eases.

There are any number of reasons your mother might not be in your life. Perhaps she has died, your father and mother divorced, she went to prison, she gave you up for adoption or she became addicted to drugs or alcohol. If your mother is still alive, the good news is that even though you may have feelings of anger or disappointment, there is hope that she might one day be in your life again.

It may not be easy, and no one knows what the result will be, but if she is alive there is hope.

After my mother died, I wondered almost all of the time, what would happen to me. I didn't know what kind of life or future I would have. I didn't think I was special or good or nice or pretty. I had a lot of hopes and dreams but they seemed so far away and unreachable. I was sad even when others were around. I didn't speak much because I thought other people would think what I said was stupid and because I did not like the sound of my voice.

It has been many, many years since my mother passed away. As the years went by, I grew from being a five year girl without a mom, to a teenager who struggled to make friends so spent most of my time reading books in libraries, to becoming a college graduate, corporate vice president, writer, wife, mother and public speaker.

Even though the beginning of my life started out with pain and sadness, I am now very happy and content. Believe me when I tell you that you can, if you choose, overcome the sadness of not having your mother in your life, and live a life filled with joy. Will it always be easy? No. Will you sometimes want to give up? Maybe. Will you miss your mom? Most definitely. Can you find reasons to smile during the day? Yes. Can your heart ever be filled with goodness and gladness? Yes. Does anyone in this world care about you? Yes! Can you have a present and a future with hope and success?

Yes. Yes. Yes.

As you walk down the pathways of your life, you will have many different experiences. Some will be encouraging and easily move you forward, while others may make you question if you should continue at all.

Whatever you do, keep living your life. Never give up. Put one foot in front of the other and never stop living, loving and learning. It won't always be easy but it's not always easy for anyone. Yet, still, life can be a wonderful, exciting journey for those who decide they will press on no matter what.

I would like to offer you a few gifts to take with you on your travels. I hope you don't put them in a suitcase and close them up but keep them near to your heart so that when you're facing a steep hill that seems impossible to mount, they will help you to keep on climbing. What are the gifts? They are words, hugs, love and encouragement from me, a mother who knows what it's like to not have a mother. They are words that so many mothers would say to their children if they could. Words that some mothers may want to say but do not know how. Words that maybe, just maybe, your heart and ears are longing to hear.

Special one, these words are for you.

Whispers To Your Heart

You Were Created
You Are Loved
Finding Friends
Smile With Joy
Dating Do's and Dating Don'ts
Here's to Healthy
A Word About Money
Every Day Thanksgivings
Never Give Up
A Beautiful Life

Remarkable Creation

You, you know are one of a kind.
Created by God, with a heart, soul and mind.
With His hand and breath He made you alive -
Fashioned and formed for good things to strive.
Do not listen to what can't be done,
You were created by love, you've already won.
Get ready, be prepared for any test,
You have what it takes so give it your best.
On the days when it's hard, continue to try,
Reach, stretch, your palms to the sky.
Be respectful, kind and caring along the way,
for opportunities called challenges are training.

1
You Were Created

Create: (1)to cause to come into being, as something unique that would not naturally evolve or that is not made by ordinary processes. (2) to evolve from an imagination, as a work of art or an invention.

If you are near a mirror or anything that can show your reflection, stand in front of it and look closely at your face. What do you see? Two eyes. A nose. A mouth. Two ears. Skin. I can only imagine how beautiful your eyes must be. Perhaps they are as beautifully brown as an oak tree , or as awe inspiring and blue as a spring morning sky. Your eyes were created and designed to fit your face. The color, size, and shape of your eyes would not fit anyone else's face as perfectly as they fit yours. They were made for you.

Focus for a few seconds on one of your eyes. There is an eyelid. The eyelid has eyelashes. The eyeball contains a cornea, an iris, and a pupil. Each part of your eye has a special function. Your eyelids protect and moisten your eye. Eyelashes help to keep particles from getting into your eyes. The cornea's job is to focus light coming into it. The iris is the colorful part of the eye and its purpose is to control how much light goes through to the pupil. The pupil is the black circle in the center of the iris that allows light into the eye. The pupil adjusts to the amount of light entering it by getting smaller when light is shining close to it and getting bigger when light decreases.

Your eyes are beautiful to be sure, and they, just like every other part of you, are intricately designed. If you are still in front of a mirror, look at your ears. Notice your hair. Touch your skin. Take a look at your fingers. Straighten your shoulders. Shake your wrists. Smile and show your teeth. Continue to look at yourself in the mirror and think about the parts of yourself which you cannot see – your brain, your heart, your lungs, your blood, and your spine. They too, have been purposefully created. Whenever you look at yourself, you should realize that you are a wonderfully designed creation.

If you have been designed, then who is The Designer? Your mother and father are the people through whom you were brought to the earth, but they did not decide how tall you would be, the color of your hair, or the shape of your head. It was God, the Creator of the earth and all that is in the earth, who decided when, where and how you would be born. None of the billions of people that have ever been born or that ever will be born have had or will ever have, your DNA (the genes that make you who you are). Your fingerprints belong to you and you alone.

When God made you, He created a unique person. He imagined you in His mind, then formed you according to His plan and design. Everything about your birth is on purpose – who your parents are, the city you were born in and the day you were born on. They are all exactly as God intended.

If you feel special, it is because you are special. You were created by the same God that created the sky, the ocean, the moon, the stars, water, oxygen, butterflies, lions, dogs and everything else in heaven and earth.

Here is what God says:

"And even the very hairs of your head are all numbered."

Matthew 10:30

"For by him all things were created: things in heaven and on earth, visible and invisible, whether thrones or powers or rulers or authorities; all things were created by him and for him."

Colossians 1:16

"For you created my inmost being; you knit me together in my mother's womb."

Psalm 139:13

A place for your thoughts

The One

God created you.
God knows you.
God sees you.
God cares for you.
God is with you.
God hears you.
God loves you

2

You Are Loved

Love: (1) a feeling of warm personal attachment or deep affection, as for a parent, child, or friend. (2) affectionate concern for the well-being of others.

Living without your mother and her love may make you wonder if anyone in this world loves you. If you have ever asked that question before, the answer is yes.

You can be sure that you are loved. God created you because He loves you. I am writing to you because I love you. I love you because I know what it feels like to not have a mother look you in your eyes and tell you how beautiful you are or make you feel better when someone hurts your feelings.

You are loved unconditionally. You are loved because of who you are not because of what you do, where you were born or what you look like. Your height, your school performance, where you live, the things you own, the length of your hair and the color of your skin, have no effect on how much you are loved.

It is a sad fact of life that people can say things that are very hurtful. Just remember that negative, harmful words others say have nothing to do with who you are.

If you are ever feeling unloved, remember:
Sunsets, roses, butterflies, changing colors of fall leaves, and puppies are all amazing creations of God. You, however, are His greatest masterpiece.
You never have to feel small or believe you do not matter. You are invaluable and irreplaceable.

Love yourself. Go easy on yourself. You will not do everything perfectly, and that is ok. Learn the lessons your mistakes are meant to teach you so you can understand how to do better the next time. God gives us plenty of second chances. When critical words about yourself come to mind, push them out and replace them with the truth -- that you are God's masterpiece and nothing can ever change that.

Love your life. Dance, sing, play and laugh like nobody's watching. Keep your sense of wonder about the world. Accept the love friends and family will offer you. Hold on to hope and believe in the tomorrow God has planned for you.

Dear special one, I know there will be times when you will miss the safety of your mother's arms. I understand there will be days when you would give anything just to touch her face or have her touch yours. And I know that there will be almost nothing anyone can say to take away the ache in your heart of knowing that she is not with you. On those days please know that I know how you feel and through these words I am sending you a mother's hug and love.

But even more than that, on difficult days, find a time to kneel and talk to God. Tell Him whatever is on your heart. He will listen. He cares for you. Ask other Christian family members and friends to pray with and for you. You are not alone. You are loved very, very much.

Never doubt it.

Here is what God says:

"But the eyes of the LORD are on those who fear him, on those whose hope is in his unfailing love,"

Psalm 33:18

"Your love, O LORD, reaches to the heavens, your faithfulness to the skies."

Psalm 36:5

"I will be glad and rejoice in your love, for you saw my affliction and knew the anguish of my soul.

Psalm 31:7

"Love never fails."

Corinthians 13:8

"And now these three remain: faith, hope and love. But the greatest of these is love. "

1 Corinthians 13:13

"May your unfailing love rest upon us, O LORD, even as we put our hope in you."

Psalm 33:22

"Turn, O LORD, and deliver me; save me because of your unfailing love."

Psalm 6:4

"Love is patient, love is kind. It does not envy, it does not boast, it is not proud."

1 Corinthians 13:4

"Love does not delight in evil but rejoices with the truth."

1 Corinthians 13:6

Your thoughts about love

When You Need a Friend

The one who says,
"I am your friend -
my shoulder, my ear,
I have to lend.
You can always count on me -
here for you
is where I promise to be."
is one you can call
a friend in deed!

3
Finding Friends

Friend: (1) a person attached to another by feelings of affection or personal regard. (2) a person who gives assistance; patron; supporter (3) a person who is on good terms with another; a person who is not hostile.

Having friends is one of life's great pleasures. A friend inspires you to grow, to dream, to develop a good character and live with integrity. Friends bring out the best in you. With a friend you can laugh at nothing at all or at absolutely everything. You can be silly or serious with a friend. A friend lets you cry on their shoulder and locks all of your deepest secrets in their heart.

Choose your friends very carefully. Not everyone you meet will make a good friend. Watch out for anyone who always wants something from you. If you have a friend that you are always giving things to, and who never gives you anything in return, you need to consider whether or not he or she has your best interests at heart. Friendship should not be based on one person always giving to the other.

A true friend wants the best for you and will tell you the truth, whether or not you want to hear it. They may study with you, help you to make good moral decisions and encourage you to achieve your dreams and goals. Someone you consider a friend who suggests for you to participate in harmful behaviors like doing drugs or drinking alcohol is not a friend.

A real friend's heart will be hurt if you engaged in behavior that would damage or dishonor your body. What does it take to be a good friend? You should be humble, polite and respectful. Do not repeat rumors or gossip about other friends. Accept your friends for who they are.

Treat your friends the way you want to be treated. Do not betray the trust of a friend unless keeping silent would mean someone might get hurt. In such an instance you should confide in a responsible adult.

Friends are a blessing from God. I pray that you choose friends that will love, encourage and support you to become and be your very best and that you would be the same type of friend to others.

Here is what God says:

"A righteous man is cautious in friendship, but the way of the wicked leads them astray."

Proverbs 12:26

"A perverse man stirs up dissension, and a gossip separates close friends."

Proverbs 16:28

"Do not make friends with a hot-tempered man, do not associate with one easily angered,"

Proverbs 22:24

"A man of many companions may come to ruin, but there is a friend who sticks closer than a brother."

Proverbs 18:24

Thoughts on Friendship

Dance Your Shooby Doo

I know it is hard,
I've been there too;
when you wonder who's gonna teach you
to dance the shooby doo.
you wanna slap and scream
and shout your pain
but even after you do,
the feelings stay the same.
"what's the use?" taunts a voice in your head -
listen to me child, look ahead instead.
but no one understands
you think and you cry:
"what did I do to have a mommy
who said goodbye?"
You think it should rain, be cold and wet
so that others too would stay in and fret.
listen to me child, forget the fret,
open your hands,
receive what's to get.
you say,
"The air is heavy, the sun a bit dull,

what others call music
to me is a noisy lull."
How can anyone tell a joke
or dance the night away
when without your mother
every day is gray?
listen to me child, say to gray,
"Life is for living –
I will find joy today."
I know it is hard - I've been there too;
come on, turn up the music,
let's dance the shooby doo.

4
Smile With Joy

Joy: The emotion of great delight or happiness caused by something exceptionally good or satisfying; keen pleasure; elation.

Do you think it is possible to live with joy every day? Many people have days where they might not feel like getting out of bed, eating, or going outside. Even in such a day, joy can still be found. You can remember that there is a God who created this world and all of life for good purposes and although you might not understand why certain experiences have come your way, God knows why, and you can lean on, trust and hope in Him, through everything and anything.

The God who created you wants you to experience and live with joy.

That does not mean you are to walk around smiling and pretending that everything feels great all the time. What it does mean, is that in spite of the pain and sadness you may sometimes experience, He wants you to remember that with Him, there's always reasons to be hopeful.

Seeing beyond your circumstances to find joy is only possible by focusing on God throughout your life's experiences. Always remember that you can open your heart and talk to God about anything. You can ask Him to give you peace. You can ask Him how to handle what you are feeling in your heart.

What is it that gives you joy and makes your heart smile? Is it seeing your friends? Watching the sun rise? Singing your favorite song? Reading poetry? Looking at pictures of people you love? There is something I'm sure that fills your heart with gladness. Whatever it is, thank

God for it. If singing brings you joy, sing loud and often.

If you have friends that give you great advice and help you through life, thank God, and thank them for being your friend. If listening to music makes you dance, turn the volume up. If watching the stars at night or the sun rise in the morning, fills you with awe, let the Lord who created them know how thankful you are that He made these wonders for your eyes to enjoy. If writing or reading settles your soul, read or write the words that stir you.

Is it possible to live every day with a sense of joy? Yes. There will days when finding a reason to be joyful might not be too easy. Prepare for those days by reserving a place in your heart for God's words that you have memorized to encourage you. Agree with a friend that you can call him or her to have a good laugh, or pick up this book and re-read this section.

I pray that you live your life seeking to discover the joy that can be found with the God who knows your yesterday, today and tomorrow.

Here is what God says:

"The LORD is my strength and my shield; my heart trusts in him, and I am helped. My heart leaps for joy and I will give thanks to him in song."

Psalm 28:7

"Sing to him a new song; play skillfully, and shout for joy."

Psalm 33:3

"The LORD has done great things for us, and we are filled with joy."

Psalm 126:3

"A cheerful look brings joy to the heart, and good news gives health to the bones."

Proverbs 15:30

"When anxiety was great within me, your consolation brought joy to my soul."

Psalm 94:19

What gives you joy?

Do the Right Thing

Sometimes it's hard to do the right thing
Who knows the teases and taunts
it might bring?
Others perhaps will say
you're not cool;
Yes, it's true some folks
can be cruel.
But do the right thing
any way,
You will certainly be glad you did,
one day

.

5
Dating Do's & Don'ts

Date: (1) An engagement to go out socially with another person, a connection, association, or involvement.

There will, or perhaps already has come, a time when you will want to start dating. The purpose of dating should be to discover how to become friends with and learn about a person of the opposite gender whom you find interesting.

When dating is done the right way it can become the way you find the person you will one day marry and start a family with. Special one, dating should never be used to become emotionally involved with someone in ways that dishonors you, your body, or another person. That is dangerous territory.

Hopefully you have adults in your life that can guide and teach you how to date since breaking a dating relationship can be very painful if the two people allowed themselves to get too emotionally involved with each other. You should understand the reasons why you want to date a particular person and get the opinion of other responsible adults in your life.

One of the best reasons to begin dating someone is because you believe that you will be friends for many years to come and that the person has the qualities to make a great spouse one day. Before you start to date, make a list of the qualities and characteristics that are acceptable and unacceptable to you in a potential dating partner. Pray to God and ask Him to give you the wisdom to recognize good and poor qualities.

You will get to know your dating partner just as you would get to know any friend, which is by talking. Ask a lot of questions. What are their beliefs about God? What are their views on marriage? What are their potential career choices? Do they like to spend or save money? In what ways do they honor their mother and father? What are their beliefs regarding remaining pure and honorable until marriage? Do they like cats, dogs or neither?

Talking reveals the true qualities and characteristics of a person. The more you have in common with your dating friend, the longer you will remain friends and the better your future relationship will be, if you decide to get married one day. You should also pray for God to give you the strength to avoid investing too much emotion into a long term friendship, and that He helps you to remain firm in your commitment to stay pure and honorable until the day you marry. You can pray by yourself or with others. The potential pain of a broken heart because of dating mistakes is too risky to not pray about them.

Dating relationships should be based on respect. Words spoken to each other should be wholesome, encouraging and used to build one another up. Disrespectful words are a clear warning sign of other disrespectful behavior to follow. Respect includes honoring the boundaries you have set up for yourself. If you have (which I hope you have) decided that you will keep yourself pure until you are married, then this needs to be respected by your dating friend.

To help you keep your vow of purity until marriage, avoid being alone at home or other private places without others around. Go on group dates. Seeing how your dating friend interacts with your family and friends is another way to get insight into a person's character. A dating partner should never pressure you to walk away from your values. A true friend will honor your commitment to remain pure.

Special one, be careful of dating too many people. It is best to save dating relationships for the few people who have the best potential of making a great spouse. Having a trail of ex-dating friends may make it more difficult to have a strong, healthy marriage in the future. Breaking off dating relationships hurts and having your heart broken too many times may cause you to mistrust other people.

Above all, keep God at the center of your life. Put your complete trust in Him and not in another person. If you do this, you will be able to guard and protect your heart until you meet the person who will be your lifetime spouse.

Here is what God says:

"Love the LORD your God with all your heart and with all your soul and with all your strength."

Deuteronomy 6:5

"Above all else, guard your heart, for it is the wellspring of life."

Proverbs 4:23

"Flee from sexual immorality. All other sins a person commits are outside the body, but whoever sins sexually, sins against their own body.

1Corinthians 6:18

"I seek you with all my heart; do not let me stray from your commands."

Psalm 119:10

Thoughts on Dating

happy birthday every day

wherever in the world
you happen to be -
America, Ghana,
or even New Delhi,
look to the sky
dream dreams on high
you were birthed
for possibility

6
Here's To Health

Health: (1) the general condition of the body or mind with reference to soundness (2) soundness of body or mind; freedom from disease or ailment:

It's no fun being sick. If you have ever had a cold, the flu, a stomach virus, or even a headache you know how unpleasant it is. You might have a fever, chills or body aches. One thing is for sure, when you are sick all you want to do is get better. Homework assignments do not get done, book reading does not happen, and there is no going outside. A mother will usually do all that is within her power to bring one of her sick children back to health. It makes a mother's heart ache to watch her child suffer through sickness or pain.

So, what are some things you can do to help yourself – (and the hearts of mothers) stay healthy and happy? One of the first is to eat well.

Fruits, vegetables, and water contain many great nutrients that help strengthen the body's immune system – which is the part of our body that fights germs. You should eat fruits and vegetables and drink water as often as you can during the day.

Playing sports and staying active outdoors is another excellent way to have a healthy mind, body and spirit. There are many ways to exercise and help keep your muscles and heart strong. Walking, dancing and running are great ways to exercise. That's right – you can put on some upbeat music that you love and dance, dance, dance your body into shape! A lack of exercise can cause obesity – a very dangerous condition that can place stress and pressure on the heart. A little body movement goes a long way, and what you do today, your body will thank you for one day in the future.

Some people who do not understand how much they are loved and how valuable they are do not take very good care of themselves. Unfortunately, some even damage their bodies by drinking alcohol, doing drugs or having eating disorders. If this is where you are, you need to find a responsible adult or friend to talk to so you can get the help you need. It breaks the hearts of mothers to see their children damage their beautiful God-given mind, spirit and body.

Today is a great day to eat well and exercise. Regardless of what you did or did not do yesterday, each day is a new beginning. Love, honor and treat yourself well – and never, ever, let anyone else dishonor or harm your body. If anyone tries to hurt you– tell a trustworthy, responsible adult immediately. Remember that

God created each and every part of you and gave them to you as a gift.

Here is what God says:

"Do you not know that your body is a temple of the Holy Spirit, who is in you, whom you have received from God? You are not your own; you were bought at a price. Therefore honor God with your body."

1 Corinthians 6:19-20

"For physical training is of some value, but godliness has value for all things, holding promise for both the present life and the life to come."

1 Timothy 4:8

"A peaceful heart leads to a healthy body; jealousy is like cancer in the bones. "

Proverbs 14:30

"I praise you because I am fearfully and wonderfully made; your works are wonderful, I know that full well."

Psalm 139:14

"Come to me, all you who are weary and burdened, and I will give you rest. Take my yoke upon you and learn from me, for I am gentle and humble in heart, and you will find rest for your souls."

Matthew 11:28-29

For you created my inmost being; you knit me together in my mother's womb.

Psalm 139:13

A cheerful heart is good medicine, but a crushed spirit dries up the bones.

Proverbs 17:22

How will you stay healthy?

7
A Word About Money

Money: (1) a particular form or denomination of currency. (2) capital to be borrowed, loaned, or invested.

Money is used as a means of exchange throughout the world. The dollar is used in the United States, the cedi is used in Ghana and the peso is used in Mexico. Without money it would not be possible to get housing, food or clothing. Throughout your lifetime, you will have opportunities to earn, save and give money.

You may or may not know the type of job or career you want to have as an adult. Pray to God and ask Him to help you make the right education choices that will prepare you for work that fits the talents, skills and personality He has given you. Your chosen job or career is one of the ways you will contribute to the world and be rewarded with income.

You can earn money even before you become an adult. Different countries and states have different laws regarding the age at which a person under eighteen can work, so before you begin looking for a job or start your own business, be sure you know what those laws are. Some people choose to commit crimes and other dangerous activities to get money. You, on the other hand, should earn money only in ways that are pleasing to God.

Once you begin earning money, you should use it responsibly. The money you earn might be used for school fees, clothes, perhaps to help at home, or going to the movies. Be sure to save some of the money you earn. Try not to spend all of your money as soon as you get it. This is a habit that if carried into your future, may cause problems when trying to provide for you or your family's needs. If you develop good money habits you will be on the right track for living without owing other people (debt), be able to give to worthy ministries and organizations, and acquire wealth which you can use to make a difference in your community and pass on to your family.

Determine how you would like to contribute to the world with the gifts, skills and talents you were created with. Live honorably, responsibly and with integrity, in all that you do, including how you handle money.

Here is what God says:

"No servant can serve two masters. Either he will hate the one and love the other, or he will be devoted to the one and despise the other. You cannot serve both God and Money."

Luke 16:13

"Do not store up for yourselves treasures on earth, where moth and rust destroy, and where thieves break in and steal. But store up for yourselves treasures in heaven, where moth and rust do not destroy, and where thieves do not break in and steal. For where your treasure is, there your heart will be also."

Matthew 6:19-21

"Keep your lives free from the love of money and be content with what you have, because God has said, "Never will I leave you; never will I forsake you."

Hebrews 13:5

"The Lord sends poverty and wealth; he humbles and he exalts."

1 Sam 2:7

"I am not saying this because I am in need, for I have learned to be content whatever the circumstances. 12I know what it is to be in need, and I know what it is to have plenty. I have learned the secret of being content in any and every situation, whether well fed or hungry, whether living in plenty or in want. 13I can do everything through him who gives me strength."

Philippians 4:11-13

"But godliness with contentment is great gain. For we brought nothing into the world, and we can take nothing out of it. But if we have food and clothing, we will be content with that. People who want to get rich fall into temptation and a trap and into many foolish and harmful desires that plunge men into ruin and destruction."

1 Tim 6:6-9

"For the love of money is a root of all kinds of evil. Some people, eager for money, have wandered from the faith and pierced themselves through with many griefs. But you, man of God, flee from all this, and pursue righteousness, godliness, faith, love, endurance and gentleness."

1 Tim 6:10-12

"What good is it for a man to gain the whole world, yet lose or forfeit his very self?"

Luke 9:25

Your Thoughts on Money

Thankful

Grace

said

in front of a plate

when nothing to sup

could have been your fate.

so to God

you owe

and should live to show

thanks to Grace

and for others to know.

8
Everyday Thanksgivings

Thankful: (1) feeling or expressing gratitude; appreciative.

Some of the hardest times I ever had were seeing someone laughing, walking hand in hand or sitting on the laps of their mothers. No matter where I was when I would see a mother interacting with her son or daughter, I would stare at them and picture them as my mother and me. I imagined me sitting in her lap, laughing, smiling and happy.

At the end of my daydream realizing I was standing alone, sadness would creep into my heart or I would become angry that my mother was taken away. I could not understand why of all the people in the world I had to be the one without a mother.

Even though I did not have a mother, I had brothers, sisters, aunts, uncles and cousins. We played and laughed together every day. Sometimes we would fight and argue or scream at each other but that never lasted. By the end of the day we were in the basement singing and making up dances.

Thanksgiving at Grandma's was my favorite time of the year. I liked it better than my birthday. Just thinking about opening Grandma's front door to be welcomed by the smell of baked macaroni and cheese, cooling sweet potato pie and turkey roasting in the oven, gave me goose bumps. What was even better though, was hearing my aunts and uncles playing card games in the kitchen, or the music and laughter of my cousins coming from the basement.

My family, music and writing helped my heart the most when I thought the sadness of missing my mother was more than I could stand. During those times, instead of being alone, I could sit with my sister, brother or cousin. I could play my favorite songs or I could write how I felt in a poem or letter.

What about you? Even though your mother may not be with you, who is with you? What other things in your life do you have that calm you, bring you peace, make you laugh or sing? Whatever they are, be thankful that you have them. If you are able to enjoy music, thank God that your ears are able to hear and your heart is able to feel. There are so many other things you can be thankful for too. Are you able to eat a meal every day? Do you have a place to sleep? Clothes to wear? Are you in school? Are you able to learn?

There are today people who cannot go to school, have no idea what they will eat, or do not have a family that cares about them. Each and every day you can be thankful for things like having your life, being warmed by the sun, your eyesight, clean water, and so much more. The cure for a sad mood is to speak words of gratitude.

Here is what God says:

"Be thankful in all circumstances, for this is God's will for you who belong to Christ Jesus."

1st Thessalonians 5:18

"I will give to the Lord the thanks due to His rightness and justice, and I will sing praise to the name of the Lord Most High."

Psalm 7: 17

Do not be anxious about anything, but in everything, by prayer and petition, with thanksgiving, present your requests to God.

Philippians 4:6

What are you thankful for?

The Good Book

Now you might think it rather funny
that a book is more valuable
than large sums of money.
how, do you ask?, is what I utter so?
just keep on reading
there's something I want you to know.
when I was but an itty bitty girl
My mom got sick
and then she left this world.
I was always sorry and sad in my home –
I had no mother, I was so alone.
nothing at all seemed as though it was right,
oh dear God, what would be my plight?
should I run? should I stay? oh it hurts so bad
to be constantly crying and all the time sad.
for love, smiles and joy I would look,
and then one day I found them in a book.
I read a story of Abraham –
to God he was a very special man.
I also read of Noah and his friends –

that one I read again and again.
and so it began when I would feel sorry,
I learned to have hope and not to worry.
yes some days were full of strife,
but it was The Bible that helped my life.
so if things are tough, of this you can be sure,
God and His Words are the perfect cure.
Never give up no matter what you do,
just grab The Good Book –
it will get you through.

Never Give Up
9

Perseverance: (1) maintain a purpose in spite of difficulty, obstacles, or discouragement; continue steadfastly.

Have you ever had a difficult time completing a homework assignment, taking medicine, or some other activity? When you completed the assignment how did you feel? Did you think of yourself as a winner? Were you proud of yourself for tackling the difficult assignment through to the end? Even though the medicine may have tasted horrible, did it make you well?

Not giving up even when a situation or assignment seems impossible, is called perseverance - - and it is what life is all about.
If there is something you can be assured of, it is that you will face difficult periods in your life. If

you are without your mother at this very moment, this may be one of those tough times.
Believe me, I understand not being able to run into a mother's opened arms to be held and comforted. I know what it is like to be taunted or called names in school and wish to have your mother kiss you on the cheek or forehead to make it all better.

When you are having one of those days, hold on. Hold on to the fact that tomorrow will be a new day. Hold on to the remembrance of the success you had over past difficult days. Hold on to the fact that there are many others who faced very similar days to yours and because they were determined to persevere, they became judges, teachers, lawyers, writers, doctors, mothers, fathers, mayors, artists, singers, pastors and so much more.

Present difficulties do not predict your future. Your determination to trust God and envision a hopeful future for yourself does. Even on my loneliest days I pictured myself helping children when I became an adult. When I thought of myself as a grown up, I pictured someone who would feed and help hungry and hurting kids. And guess what? Because I stayed in school, studied and worked hard and trusted God, I have been able to have great jobs that provided me with income to do those very things over the years.

The only reason I am able to write to you about not having a mother is because I experienced it as a young person too. Maybe one day you will be able to comfort someone else because you persevered. Never give up. You will always carry the love and feelings of your mother in your heart. That's okay. Honor God, honor her, and honor yourself by determining to live the best life you can live. Look to the future. There is hope there.

Here is what God says:

" 'For I know the plans I have for you,' declares the LORD, 'plans to prosper you and not to harm you, plans to give you hope and a future.' "

Jeremiah 29:11

"Trust in the LORD with all your heart and lean not on your own understanding"

Proverbs 3:5

"Be strong and take heart, all you who hope in the LORD."

Psalms 31:24

Your Thoughts on Persistence

The Rose Lesson

To step inside is what I longed for -
but before my hands could touch the door,
the tended porch roses had something in store:
a kiss to my heart,
whispered promises to never part,
ballets of red, to store in my head.
only then would they allow me to go
into my dear Grandma's home
where music soared,
cards players roared,
good food, poured and poured.
later on,
when life
got
tough,
rose kisses and ballet lessons I began
remembering:
Yes, that cold, dense, winter mud
is fertile ground for the birth of a beautiful thing.

10

A Beautiful Life

Beautiful: (1) having beauty; having qualities that give great pleasure or satisfaction to see, hear, think about, etc.; delighting the senses or mind: (2) excellent of its kind (3) wonderful; very pleasing or satisfying..

Life is an escapade. There will be ups. There will be downs. There will be sunny days. There will be cloudy days. There will be stormy days. There will be days so full of joy you will wish they would never end. There will be twists. There will be turns. You will make wise choices. You will make poor choices. You will do the right thing. You will do the wrong thing. You will gain rewards. Consequences of poor decisions will hurt. Without the whisper of a mother's words to help guide you, the escapade might seem terrifying.

To ease any fear or anxiety you might have about your life or your future, turn to the One who created you.

God knows you. He knows your situation. He knows what you need now. He knows what you will need in the future. He is the Only One who knows everything. He is the Only One who is perfect. He created you because He loves you and He wants you to love Him. He has given all of us a map, The Bible, to help guide us on the roads of our lives.

The Bible lets us know who God is, how to have a life with Him if we choose to, and gives us promises for life today and for our futures. It is a beautiful love letter from God and if you read it, believe it and keep it in your heart, it will help you to have a beautiful life.

Other people love you, care about you and can give you good advice, but the best guidance is based on what God has told us. Life will still have challenges and be filled with some good days and some not so good days. But, it's the promises of God that will give you the strength to make it through each and every day. We are hurt and disappointed as a result of poor choices we have made. If you make good decisions you will avoid the pain that comes along with poor ones.

The first and best choice you can ever make is to believe in Almighty God. If you need help in doing that, talk to a trusted relative, teacher, or parents of a friend, about how to become a Christian and let God lead your life. You will then begin to learn how to live and make choices that will be good for you.

I pray that you let God lead your life. I pray that even though you may be living through the experience of not having your mother in your life, you believe and know you are greatly loved.

I pray you will do well in school. I pray you will treat others kindly. I pray you will trust God. I pray you will read God's love letter to you. I pray you will ask for help when you need help. I pray God will bring good, trusted adults into your life to help teach you His ways. I pray that you will pray.

I pray that you will have a beautiful life.

Here is what God says:

"But Jesus said, 'Let the children alone, and do not hinder them from coming to Me; for the kingdom of heaven belongs to such as these.'"

Matthew 19:13-15

Made in the USA
Charleston, SC
26 April 2014